Kensuke'

Classroom Questions

A SCENE BY SCENE TEACHING GUIDE

Amy Farrell

SCENE BY SCENE
ENNISKERRY, IRELAND

Scene by Scene
Enniskerry
Wicklow, Ireland.
www.scenebysceneguides.com

Kensuke's Kingdom Classroom Questions by Amy Farrell.
ISBN 978-1-910949-57-3

Contents

Chapter One
'Peggy Sue'

Summary

The narrator has decided to talk about his disappearance the night before his twelfth birthday. He has not spoken about it before because of a promise he made to Kensuke. However, he feels that now enough time has passed for him to talk about it. Also, he does not want to deceive his family and friends any longer about his disappearance, and he wants the world to know about Kensuke and what a great man he was.

Life was normal for the narrator until he was nearly eleven. He liked school and playing football with his friends. On Sundays he went dinghy sailing on the reservoir with his parents and they all loved it.

One day a letter arrived saying the brickworks was closing down, and both of his parents were being made redundant. Neither of his parents manage to get another job.

His parents' relationship suffers and they argue a lot.

One Saturday Michael finds his mother in tears. His father has gone away to arrange a move south for the family. Michael's mother does not want to move.

When they meet Michael's father next, he is grinning and happy. He takes them to see *Peggy Sue*, a dark blue yacht, their new home.

Michael's dad plans for them to sail around the world. Despite people warning against this undertaking, including Michael's gran, the family arrange their trip.

They work hard and master their yacht together. With a fully stocked ship, they set sail.

Questions

1. When did the narrator disappear?

2. Why has the narrator decided to talk about this now? How does he feel about keeping this to himself for so long?

3. What was life like before the letter came?

4. Why were Sundays special?

5. Where did the speaker's parents work?

6. What news is in the letter? What effect does this news have on the family?

7. "A creeping misery came over the house." What are things like when the narrator's parents lose their jobs?

8. How does the narrator cope with this? Do you feel sorry for him here?

9. Why does Michael's father go off?

10. What was the last straw for him? How is he feeling, do you think?

11. Why doesn't Michael's mother want to move south?

12. How does Michael's father seem when they get off the train?
     Can you explain this change?

13. Describe Peggy Sue.

14. What is your reaction to this development?

15. How does Michael's mother react to their new home?

16. What does Michael's father want to do next?
     What do you think of this plan?

17. What will Michael do about school?

18. What does Gran warn them about?

19. Who is Bill Parker?
     What is he like?
     What sailing experience does he have?

20. Do you think the family are crazy to decide on a plan like this?

21. "We were a great team."
     Do the family work well together?
     Include examples in your answer.

22. Describe Michael's parents, giving as much detail as you can.

23. What is the mood like, as this chapter ends?

Chapter Two
'Water, water everywhere'

Summary

Michael describes life on board. He and his parents are always wet and busy working.

They are glad they brought Stella, their dog, along. She is a great comfort to them when they feel seasick or scared.

Michael's parents plan his schoolwork so he will not fall behind. For English, he writes in his version of the ship's log.

Questions

1. What is life like on board the *Peggy Sue?*

2. What different jobs does Michael do?

3. Why are they glad they brought their dog, Stella, along?

4. What programme of work have Michael's parents come up with so that he does not fall behind with his schoolwork?
   Does this sound interesting to you?

5. Would you prefer Michael's education or regular school? Give reasons for your answer.

6. Does Michael find it easy or difficult to write in his log?

7. Would you like to go on an adventure like this with your family? Give reasons for your answer.

Chapter Three
'Ship's Log'

Summary

September 20 - Michael is on watch at 5 a.m. He writes about sailing through gales in the Bay of Biscay on the way to Spain. From there they head to the Azores. Michael is fed up with baked beans already.

October 11 - Michael sees Africa in the distance. They are going down its west coast before crossing the Atlantic. It is the hottest day so far. Michael has spotted flying fish. His parents have had a disagreement, about chess he thinks.

November 16 - They just left Brazil, after stopping to make repairs. Michael played football with his dad on the beach. His mum got some pictures of their trip developed.

December 25 - The family experience Christmas Day at sea. Michael gives drawings to his parents and they give him a knife. They cleaned the boat and took on supplies in Rio. Michael did a project on Napoleon when they passed St. Helena.

January 1 - They are in Cape Town, where they plan to stay for a couple of weeks and go on safari. Michael's parents are getting on really well.

February 7 - Stella went overboard in the Indian Ocean. The family struggled to rescue her, but managed to haul her on board. Michael's mother was upset by it. They are going to visit Uncle John in Perth, Australia, next.

April 3 - Michael and his parents love the open sea, but are thrilled when they sight land, in this case, Australia. Michael's mother is suffering from stomach cramps again and intends to see a doctor.

May 28 - They stayed in Australia for six weeks, visiting Uncle John's sheep farm, going horse-riding and having barbeques. Michael enjoyed it there, but is happy to be back at sea. His mother is much better now.

July 28 - It has been terribly stormy since they left Sydney. The self-steering no longer works on the boat as a cable has snapped. This means either Michael or his dad must be at the wheel at all times. His mother is very ill again. Michael and his dad have been doing the navigation, but Michael thinks they are lost.
He is steering while his parents sleep.

The log ends here.

Michael left the wheel to get Stella, using the ball to tempt her. The ball rolled away from him and went over the side, to Michael's annoyance.

Stella refused to come with him, so he picked her up.

The boat veered violently and Michael and Stella went overboard.

Questions

1. What was sailing in the Bay of Biscay like?

2. Are Michael's parents enjoying life at sea?

3. *October 11*
   Where will the family go once they are past the west coast of Africa?

4. Why do they want to avoid the Doldrums?

5. What sealife has Michael spotted so far?

6. Does this trip sound like fun to you?

7. *November 16*
   Where are the family on November 16?

8. What problems have they had on the boat?

9. Describe the football game on the beach.

10. Michael mentions some holiday photos they get developed.
    Do you have any favourite holiday pictures?

11. *December 25*
    Describe Christmas Day at sea.

12. What does Michael give his parents?

13. What gift does Michael receive?
Is this a good gift, in your view?

14. What 'housework' do they complete in Rio?

15. Why does Michael have to do a history project on Napoleon?
Does this sound interesting to you?
Do you know anything about Napoleon?

16. Are the family getting on well, do you think?
Are they having fun?

17. *January 1*
What do the family plan to do in Cape Town?
Does this sound good to you?

18. How well are Michael's parents getting on?
What is your response to this?

19. *February 7*
What happened to Stella in the Indian Ocean?
Does this sound tense to you?

20. Was it difficult to rescue Stella?

21. Why is Michael so happy?

22. *April 3*
How do the family react when they sight Australia for the first time?

23. The family have sailed halfway around the world.
Do you think this is a great achievement?

24. What is wrong with Michael's mother?
Does it sound serious?
What could be causing her illness, do you think?

25. *May 28*
What sort of farm has Uncle John?

26. What are copperheads and redback spiders?

27. Does Michael have a good time in Australia?

28. Where are they going to next?

29. *July 28*
What has the weather been like since leaving Sydney?

30. What problem are they having with the yacht?

31. How is Michael's mother?

32. Why is Michael unsure of their location?

33. What is going on as this log entry ends?

34. Why does Michael leave the wheel?

35. What happens to his ball?
Why is he so annoyed about this?

36. How does he end up going overboard?

37.   Is this an exciting place to end a chapter?
        Give reasons for your answer.

38.   What, do you think, will happen next?

39.   In this chapter, Michael records their journey, mentioning
        the places where they land.
        What is the most interesting place you have ever visited?

40.   Where would you like to go on holiday, if you could go
        anywhere in the world?
        Give reasons for your answer.

Chapter Four
'Gibbons and Ghosts'

Summary

As the *Peggy Sue* disappears, Michael is terrified with thoughts of being left behind and also of sharks.

He finds his football, but cannot find Stella in the water. He grows weaker, exhausted by the effort of staying afloat.

He drifts off and dreams that strong arms are pulling him from the water. He wakes up on a beach with Stella nearby. She barks at the howling of the gibbons in the trees.

Michael and Stella go uphill through the forest and discover that there is sea on all sides; they are on an island.

Michael reasons that he will eat and drink whatever the monkeys do, and survive that way. He goes in search of water, but finds none.

He decides to spend the night in a small cave, avoiding the jungle and its many watchful eyes.

The next morning, Michael finds Stella drinking from a bowl. He discovers another bowl of water and strips of fish and small red bananas laid out nearby.

Once he has eaten, Michael shouts thank you, but no-one emerges in response to his calls.

He finds the rusted hull of a ship sunk deep in the sand. Michael finds a piece of glass nearby, which he uses to try to start a fire.

Stella growls at an orang-utan that comes out of the forest to look at them.

Michael's fire takes hold and he gathers material to keep it going. Stella does not go into the forest when Michael gathers wood, but stays warily by the fire.

Michael comes out of the forest to discover a man scooping sand onto his fire, extinguishing it.

Questions

1. How does Michael feel when he goes overboard?
   What would you be most worried about, in his position?

2. Why does he stop calling for Stella?

3. Michael decides against swimming.
   What plan does he come up with?
   What do you think of his plan?

4. Why does Michael sing?

5. How do you know that Michael is exhausted?

6. What does Michael dream about?

7. Where does Michael wake up?

8. How does Michael react to being all alone on the beach?
   How would you feel, in his position?

9. What is making the howling noise?
   Does this tell you anything about where Michael has
   ended up?

10. What is it like in the forest?

11. Describe the island.

12. Is Michael worried about staying alive?

13. Does he have much success looking for water?

14.   What is Michael scared of as night falls?

15.   What makes it difficult to sleep?

16.   What does Stella discover the next morning?

17.   What has been laid out for Michael?
        How does he respond to this?
        What is your response?

18.   What do they discover buried in the sand?

19.   What does Michael use to try to light a fire?
        Is this an easy job?

20.   What makes Stella growl?

21.   What happens to Michael's fire as the chapter ends?
        Were you expecting something like this to happen?
        How would you feel if you were Michael?

22.   How would you illustrate this chapter?
        Explain your choice of images.

Chapter Five
'I, Kensuke'

Summary

The man is small and old, wearing only tattered trousers.

He is very angry and shouts at Michael, but Michael does not understand the language he speaks.

To Michael's surprise, Stella is friendly towards the man.

The man tells Michael that he cannot have a fire. Then he outlines a map of the island in the sand and divides it in two, telling Michael to keep to his side. He tells him his name is Kensuke.

Michael stays in his cave for the rest of the day, feeling very alone, trying to make sense of the situation he finds himself in.

The next day, Kensuke has left food and water for Michael and Stella. Michael interprets this as a signal that Kensuke will keep them alive, but will not be their friend.

Michael stays to his side of the island and begins to find fruit that he can eat, but is unsuccessful fishing.

By night, mosquitoes eat him alive.

He learns how best to avoid sunburn.

The high point of his day is swimming each afternoon with Stella, stopping only when darkness falls.

One day Michael finds that the old man has left him matting, and rolled inside it, a sheet to protect him from the mosquitoes at night.

Michael is very happy and grateful to receive this gift.

The next morning he spots a passing super-tanker from his hill-top lookout spot.

Questions

1.   Describe the man that Michael meets.

2.   Michael does not understand the language the man
     speaks.
     How does he know that the old man is angry?

3.   How does Stella react to this man?

4.   What does this man tell Michael?

5.   Why does the man draw an outline of the island in the
     sand?
     How would you feel about this, if you were Michael?
     Would you do as the man is asking?

6.   What is the man's name?

7.   Why does Michael feel let down by Stella?

8.   Why does Michael stay in his cave for the rest of the day?

9.   What makes Michael feel confused?
     Is it a confusing situation?

10. How does Michael interpret the food and water that
     Kensuke leaves for him the next morning?

11. Why does Michael stick to his side of the island?
     Would you, in his position?

12.   What does Michael eat?

13.   Why does Michael keep out of the forest?

14.   What is night on the island like for Michael?

15.   How does Michael protect himself from sunburn?

16.   What is the highlight of Michael's day?
        Does this sound good to you?

17.   What gift does the old man leave for Michael?
        Why is Michael so happy to receive it?
        Does this gesture tell you anything about the old man?

18.   Why does Michael want to see the old man so much?
        Do you understand why he feels this way?

19.   What does Michael see as the chapter ends?
        What does this mean for him?

Chapter Six
'Abunai'

Summary

Michael leaps to his feet, shouting to attract the attention of the ship. When it passes he decides to build a beacon that he can light the next time one comes.

He begins to spend his days gathering wood, building his beacon where Kensuke will not see it.

A storm hits the island and lasts for four days. Despite the weather, Kensuke leaves food and water for Michael each day.

After the storm, Michael and Stella go swimming. The old man appears. He tells them not to swim, saying it is dangerous and leads Michael out of the sea.

Michael's spirits drop and he stops going to Watch Hill, spending hours curled up in his cave each day. He is afraid to swim after Kensuke's warning.

Michael continues to construct his beacon and one morning spots a ship. He attempts to light his signal fire, but Kensuke arrives and stamps it out.

Kensuke then smashes Michael's fireglass and dismantles his beacon.

Michael goes swimming to defy the old man and is badly stung several times by jellyfish. He feels his body go rigid and expects to drown.

Questions

1.   How does Michael react to the sight of the ship?

2.   What does Michael decide as the tanker disappears from
        view?
        Does this sound like a good plan to you?

3.   How does Michael spend his days now?

4.   Describe the storm that breaks over the island.
        How would you feel at this point, if you were Michael?

5.   How would you react to being lead from the water and
        told not to swim, as Michael is here?

6.   Why does Michael find it difficult to keep his spirits up?

7.   Why does Michael hate the old man more and more?
        Do you understand what makes him feel this way?

8.   Describe the boat that Michael spots one morning.

9.   Does Michael light his beacon?
        What does Kensuke do to Michael's beacon?
        How would you react to this, if you were Michael?

10.   What do we know about Kensuke so far?

11.   Why does Michael go swimming?

12.   What happens to Michael while he is swimming?
       How is he affected by this?
       Does this sound very painful to you?

13.   How would you illustrate this chapter?
       Give reasons for the images you choose.

Chapter Seven
'All that silence said'

Summary

Michael smells vinegar on waking and thinks that he is at home. He is in a cave, but not his own one. He cannot move and his skin feels scalded.

Kensuke nurses him and over time his health improves.

Kensuke spends hours every day painting, but never shows Michael the finished work.

Kensuke keeps his cave house uncluttered, clean and tidy.

One day Kensuke shows Michael a painting of a tree in blossom and tells him that he is Japanese. After that, he shows Michael his paintings.

Michael's paralysis passes and he begins to spend more time with Kensuke and learns to spear fish.

Kensuke has a vast knowledge of the forest and where to find fruit.

One evening a young orang-utan climbs into Michael's lap and after that the older ones touch him from time to time.

Up to now, Michael and Kensuke have used few words to communicate, using mostly gestures and pictures. There is a lot that Michael wants to know about the old man.

Their days are busy and routine. What Michael enjoys best of all is watching Kensuke paint. He learns a lot about drawing and painting from the old man.

Michael admires Kensuke's skill as a craftsman. He is impressed that Kensuke makes everything he uses himself, even his orang-utan hair paintbrushes.

One rainy day, Kensuke asks Michael to teach him to speak English. Michael begins talking as they go through their days and Kensuke is a fast learner.

Kensuke asks Michael to tell him his life story and promises to return the favour.

They go fishing in a dug-out canoe and Kensuke gives Michael his football. It was in the boat.

Questions

1. Where does Michael wake up?

2. What condition is Michael in?

3. What does Kensuke do to look after Michael?

4. Describe Kensuke's cave.
    Does it sound well-equipped to you?
    What does it reveal to you about Kensuke's character?

5. What does the first painting he shows to Michael tell you about Kensuke?

6. What does Michael start to do, once the paralysis passes?

7. How has life improved for Michael since being stung by the jellyfish?

8. Does Kensuke know the island well?
    Give examples to support your answer.

9. Are you surprised by the way the orang-utans follow Kensuke?
    How does he call them?

10. How have Michael and Kensuke communicated up to now?

11.   How do Michael and Kensuke spend their time?
       Is this lifestyle appealing to you?

12.   Why does Michael enjoy watching Kensuke paint?

13.   What does Michael learn about drawing and painting
       from Kensuke?

14.   How does Kensuke make his paintbrushes?
       Are you impressed by his resourcefulness here?

15.   What does Kensuke want Michael to teach him?

16.   How does Michael teach Kensuke?

17.   Is Kensuke a good student?
       Give reasons for your answer.

18.   What does Kensuke keep hidden on the beach?

19.   What item does Kensuke return to Michael?
       How would you feel, if you were Michael?

20.   How has their relationship changed and developed since
       Michael's arrival on the island?
       Can you explain these changes?

21.   What would life on the island be like for Michael, without
       Kensuke?

22.   What would life on the island be like for Kensuke,
       without Michael?

Chapter Eight
'Everyone Dead in Nagasaki'

Summary

Michael is happy to get his ball back.

Kensuke explains that the small fish are not very plentiful at this time, so they need to go fishing to catch and smoke bigger fish in order to maintain their food supply.

Once they are on the water, Kensuke tells Michael the details of his life. He was a doctor with a wife and son before war broke out and he joined the navy.

His ship was bombed and he was the only one to survive it.

He heard news on the radio, telling of the atomic bomb in Nagasaki and assumed that his family were all dead.

When a storm brought his ship to the island, he decided to stay there.

Once, American soldiers came to the island, but Kensuke hid from them in the forest with the orang-utans.

Kensuke learned to survive through watching the orang-utans.
Kensuke tells Michael about a time about a year ago when killer men came
to the island. Kensuke gathered the orang-utans and hid them in his cave,
but the men killed many gibbons and took their babies.

This made Kensuke hate all people and not want to see any again.

Kensuke explains how he rescued Michael and Stella the night Michael fell
overboard. He says that he stayed away from Michael because he was so
angry with people and did not want anyone to come to the island to harm
the animals.

He talks about Michael being stung by the dangerous jellyfish and finishes by
saying that now they are good friends, happy together, a family.

Michael agrees with Kensuke, but thinks also of his grieving parents and
longs to see them. Michael considers taking Kensuke's boat and rowing
away, but knows he could never betray his friend like this.

He finds a plastic Coke bottle and writes a note for his parents. He throws
the bottle into the sea, unknownst to Kensuke. Michael feels guilty, but also
excited at the prospect of being found.

The next day, Stella comes into the cave and drops the Coke bottle on the
ground.

Questions

1. Why does Kensuke take Michael fishing in the canoe?

2. What was Kensuke's life like as a young man?

3. What made Kensuke join the navy?

4. Describe Kensuke's war experience.

5. Why was Kensuke so sad to hear that an atomic bomb fell on Nagasaki?

6. How did Kensuke come to be on the island?

7. What did Kensuke do when American soldiers came to the island?
    Can you explain his actions here?

8. What different things did Kensuke learn from the orang-utans?

9. What does Kensuke tell Michael about the killer men?
    What is your reaction to this?

10. Why did these men do this?

11. How did their actions affect Kensuke?

12. Why was Kensuke out at sea the night that Michael fell overboard?

What state were Michael and Stella in when Kensuke found them?

13.   What made Kensuke stay away from Michael at first? Do you understand why he felt this way?

14.   Is Kensuke very honest when he tells Michael his story? Use examples to support your answer.

15.   Kensuke says that Michael is like a son to him. How does reading this make you feel?

16.   Is Michael content to remain on the island with Kensuke? What would you do, in his position?

17.   What is the significance of Michael finding a plastic Coke bottle?

18.   What do you think of Michael's note?

19.   Is there anything else you would include?

20.   Why does Michael make sure that Kensuke does not see him throwing the bottle into the sea?

21.   How does Michael's secretiveness make him feel?

22.   What makes the ending of this chapter so tense?

23.   How would you feel if you were Michael?

24.   How would you feel if you were Kensuke?

Chapter Nine
'The Night of the Turtles'

Summary

Kensuke is hurt by Michael's Coke bottle message. The pair are not as close anymore, each in his own world. Michael passes more time alone.

One night, Tomodachi, the orang-utan, comes and looks into their cave. Kensuke explains that she is looking for her baby and says that she makes him think of Michael's mother.

Kensuke understands why Michael wants to leave the island, even though he himself wants to stay and will miss Michael.

He knows that Michael has his whole life ahead of him, and so he tells Michael they will build a new fire the next day.

When the firewood is collected they spend a fun afternoon playing football together.

Kensuke's English is improving and he tells Michael stories when they go fishing together. His favourite topic is his wife and son.

Michael tries to persuade Kensuke to leave with him if a boat should come, but Kensuke insists that he wants to remain on the island.

Kensuke enjoys listening to Michael talk about Japan, despite Michael's limited knowledge.

Kensuke wakes Michael one night so that they can help newly hatched turtles safely make their way to the sea.

Kensuke admires the turtles' bravery, swimming into the unknown, and resolves to leave with Michael when the time comes.

Questions

1. How does Michael's message in the Coke bottle change his relationship with Kensuke?

2. Why does Tomodachi come to Kensuke's cave?

3. What does Tomodachi make Kensuke think of?

4. Is Kensuke a very understanding man?
   Use examples in your answer.

5. What has Kensuke decided to do the following day?

6. How do they spend the afternoon?
   Do they enjoy themselves?

7. What different things does Kensuke talk to Michael about?
   What is your response to this?

8. Why does Michael talk to Kensuke about the outside world?

9. Why does Kensuke wake Michael up one night?

10. What different things do they do to help the turtles?

11. Would you like to experience something like this?
    Give reasons for your answer.

12. What lesson do the turtles teach Kensuke?

13.   How does Kensuke's decision make you feel?

14.   Would you want to stay on the island or leave, if you were Kensuke?
Explain your answer fully.

Chapter Ten
'Killer Men Come'

Summary

The rains come, forcing Michael and Kensuke to shelter in the cave house for days. They spend a lot of their time painting.

One day a boat appears. Michael wants to light his signal fire, but Kensuke recognises the boat as that of the killer men. He and Michael gather all of the orang-utans, bar one they cannot find, and bring them to the cave for safety.

As shots ring out, Kensuke sings to the orang-utans to reassure them.

Afterwards, Kensuke is extremely upset to discover the bodies of two dead gibbons, but luckily Kikanbo, the wayward orang-utan, turns up safe and sound.

Kensuke is anxious that the hunters may return and fashions a secure cage in his cave for the orang-utans should this happen.

One morning, while collecting shells for painting, the pair spy a boat. Michael lights the beacon and eventually the boat comes towards them. This boat turns out to be the *Peggy Sue*.

Kensuke decides to stay on the island. He says that he would be like a ghost returning home if he went back to Japan. Also, he wants to protect the orang-utans.

He makes Michael promise not to say anything about him for ten years.

Michael goes to meet his parents. They are delighted to find him, after searching for a year. Everyone believed Michael to be dead, everyone except his mother.

Questions

1. Describe what it is like when the rains come.
   How do Michael and Kensuke spend their time?

2. Kensuke leaves the faces indistinct when he paints his wife and son.
   Why does he do this?
   How does this make you feel?

3. What begins to trouble Michael?

4. How does Kensuke react when Michael sees a boat?

5. How do they gather the orang-utans?

6. Why is Kensuke so upset when the killer men leave?

7. What does Kensuke do to make the orang-utans more secure in future?
   What does this tell you about his character?

8. How do Kensuke and Michael react on the next occasion when a boat approaches the island?

9. How do you feel when you learn that this boat is the *Peggy Sue?*

10. What reasons does Kensuke have for staying on the island?

11.   What three things does Kensuke make Michael promise
       him?
       What is your reaction to this?

12.   Describe Michael's reunion with his parents.

13.   What must the past year have been like for them?

14.   How do you feel as this chapter ends?
       What makes this part of the story emotional?

15.   Is Kensuke doing the right thing by choosing to stay on
       the island, in your view?

16.   What illustrations would you choose to accompany this
       chapter? Give reasons for your answer.

Postscript

Summary

Michael received a letter from Kensuke's son four years after publishing his story.

Michael went to Japan to meet him and talk about Kensuke.

Questions

1. Who is this letter from?

2. How does reading this make you feel?

3. Are you glad that Michael went to meet Michiya? Explain your answer.

4. Do you like this ending? Give reasons for your answer. Does it complete the story?

Further Questions

1.   Why is this novel called *Kensuke's Kingdom,* and not *Michael's Journey,* or something else?
Give reasons for your answer.

2.   Could you have kept this story to yourself for ten years, as Michael's character did?
Explain your answer fully.

3.   Describe Michael's character, using examples from the text to support your ideas.

4.   Describe Kensuke's character, using examples from the text to support your ideas.

5.   In what ways are Michael and Kensuke similar to each other?

6.   Describe the relationship between Michael and Kensuke.

7.   Describe the time and place this story is set in (the world of the novel).
What is appealing about this time and place?
What is unappealing about it?
Include examples in your answer.

8.   What are the main themes/issues in this novel?
Include examples in your answer.

9.   What different elements of the story combine to make this novel exciting?

10.   Who is your favourite character?
What do you like or admire about them?

11.   Which character do you dislike most?
Explain what makes you dislike them.

12.   Was there anything in the story that you would have liked to know more about?
Explain your answer, using examples.

13.   Is this a good adventure story?
Why/why not?
Explain your answer fully.

14.   Would this story make a good movie?
Which actors would you choose to play the lead roles?
Explain your choices.

15.   Did this novel teach you anything about survival?
Do you think you could survive on a remote island, like Michael and Kensuke did?
What would pose the biggest challenge in this situation?

16.   What does this story teach us about friendship?

17.   What is your favourite section of the story?
       Why did this part appeal to you?

18.   What is the saddest section of the story?
       What makes it sad and moving?

19.   What do you like about this novel?
       Give examples in your answer.

20.   What do you dislike about this novel?
       Give examples in your answer.

21.   Does this novel remind you of any other novels or films?
       Explain your view.

22.   What cover design would you choose for this novel?
       Give reasons for your answer.

23.   Would you recommend this novel to a friend?
       Why/why not?

CLASSROOM QUESTIONS GUIDES

Books of questions, designed to save teachers time and lead to rewarding classroom experiences.

www.SceneBySceneGuides.com

Printed in Great Britain
by Amazon